This Year You
Write Your Novel

Also by Walter Mosley

This Year You Write Your Novel

Walter Mosley

Little, Brown and Company
New York   Boston   London

Little, Brown and Company
Hachette Book Group USA
237 Park Avenue, New York, NY 10169
Visit our Web site at www.HachetteBookGroupUSA.com

First Edition: April 2007

Library of Congress Cataloging-in-Publication Data
Mosley, Walter.
   This year you write your novel / Walter Mosley. — 1st ed.
      p. cm.
   Includes bibliographical references.
   ISBN 978-0-316-06541-2
   1. Fiction — Authorship.   2. Fiction — Technique.   I. Title.
PN3355.M68 2007
808.3—dc22   2006035862

                    10 9 8 7 6 5 4 3 2 1

                              Q-FF

              Printed in the United States of America

In memory of William Matthews

Contents

Contents

Contents

This Year You Write Your Novel

Introduction

I'm writing this book as a guide for anyone who wishes to commit themselves to the task of beginning and completing a novel within a year's time. Here I will give you all the knowledge I have about writing, and rewriting, fiction.

Writing a novel is not nearly as difficult as some people would make it out to be. Anyone who communicates verbally, or by sign, is a writer of sorts. Any manager, mother, counselor, teacher, or guy who hangs out on the corner telling tall tales is a writer-in-waiting.

What I will try to point out in the following pages is how you can redirect your natural abilities at communication into creative prose.

But before we begin our journey, I have to present you with a few caveats concerning the goal.

First, I am fairly certain that anyone who reads this book, and who applies its lessons with tenacity, will be able to produce a complete draft of a *short* novel. I emphasize the word "short" because I doubt if many first-time novelists will be able to complete a draft of some equivalent to *Bleak House* or *War and Peace* within the requisite time. I don't promise a masterpiece, just a durable first novel of a certain length (let us say fifty to sixty thousand words).

Second, I am not promising that you will, necessarily, produce a book that is destined to be snapped up by the publishing world. It may be that you have the right story and the right words to interest a publisher. It might be that you have written a beautiful piece that no one is interested in. And, of course, your first attempt as a fiction writer might not come up to the standard set by the industry.

I can't promise you worldly success, but I can say that if you follow the path I lay out here, you will experience the personal satisfaction of having written a novel. And from that point, anything is possible.

The body of this book is broken up into five essential sections. It starts out with the general disciplines and attitudes that a writer of fiction must adopt. These practices will see you past many of the emotional, intellectual, and psychological restraints that come to bear on almost every writer.

Next I will give an exhaustive explanation of the elements of fiction writing. Here I will talk about plot and story, character and character development, showing versus telling, and narrative voice. This section will be capped off with a discussion of poetry and how important that discipline is to any writer. These are the tools of the writer of fiction; without them, the story you wish to tell will lose its way and founder.

After presenting you with these tools, I will give you some choices about how you might start your book. I will also talk about the process of writing, explaining how to create a first draft—pretty much painlessly.

After learning how to go about writing and studying the tools with which to accomplish this task, you will find out about editing, which is another term for rewriting. Rewriting is the most important job for the novelist; this is where the real work begins. The first draft is little more than an outline of the novel you wish to write. Rewriting is where you make the story into song.

After this music lesson, we talk about the miscellaneous topics of genre, publishing, and aesthetics.

Once you read these few pages, I believe that you will be prepared to write a book of your own. From that point on, all you'll need is the desire and the will to write your novel.

The General Disciplines That Every Writer Needs

writing every day

The first thing you have to know about writing is that it is something you must do every day—every morning or every night, whatever time it is that you have. Ideally, the time you decide on is also the time when you do your best work.

There are two reasons for this rule: getting the work done and connecting with your unconscious mind.

If you want to finish this novel of yours within a year, you have to get to work! There's not a moment to lose. There's no time to wait for inspiration. Getting your words down on the page takes time. How much? I write three hours every morning. It's the first thing I do, Monday through Sunday, fifty-two weeks a year. Some days I miss but rarely does this happen more than once a month. Writing is a serious enterprise that takes a certain amount of constancy and rigor.

But will and regularity are only the beginnings of the discipline and rewards that daily writing will mean for you.

The most important thing I've found about writing is that it is primarily an unconscious activity. What do I mean by this? I mean that a novel is larger than your head (or conscious mind). The connections, moods, metaphors, and experiences that you call up while writing will come from a place deep inside you. Sometimes you will wonder who wrote those words. Sometimes you will be swept up by a fevered passion relating a convoluted journey through your protagonist's ragged heart. These moments are when you have connected to some deep place within you, a place that harbors the zeal that made you want to write to begin with.

The way you get to this unconscious place is by writing every day. Or not even writing. Some days you may be rewriting, rereading, or just sitting there scrolling back and forth through the text. This is enough to bring you back into the dream of your story.

What, you ask, is the dream of a story? This is a mood and a continent of thought below your conscious mind — a place that you get closer to with each foray into the words and worlds of your novel.

You may have spent only an hour and a half working on

the book, but the rest of the day will be rife with motive moments in your unconsciousness—moments in your mind, which will be mulling over the places your words have touched. While you sleep, mountains are moving deep within your psyche. When you wake up and return to the book, you will be amazed by the realization that you are further along than when you left off yesterday.

If you skip a day or more between your writing sessions, your mind will drift away from these deep moments of your story. You will find that you'll have to slog back to a place that would have been easily attained if only you wrote every day.

Some days you will sit down and nothing will come—that's all right. Some days you'll wish you had given yourself more time—that's okay too. You can always pick up tomorrow where you left off today.

In order to be a writer, you have to set up a daily routine. Put aside an amount of time (not less than an hour and a half) to sit with your computer or notebook. I know that this is difficult. Some of you live in tight spaces with loved ones. Some of you work so hard that you can't see straight half the time. Some of you have little ones who might need your attention at any time of the day or night.

I wish I had the answers to these problems. I don't. All I can tell you is that if you want to finish your novel this year, you have to write each and every day.

learning how to write without restraint

Self-restraint is what makes it possible for society to exist. We refrain, most of the time, from expressing our rage and lust. Most of us do not steal or murder or rape. Many words come into our minds that we never utter — even when we're alone. We imagine terrible deeds but push them out of our thoughts before they've had a chance to emerge fully.

Almost all adult human beings are emotionally restrained. Our closest friends, our coworkers, and our families never know the brutal and deviant urges and furies that reside in our breasts.

This restraint is a good thing. I know that my feelings are often quite antisocial. Sometimes I just see someone walking down the street and the devil in me wants to say things that would be awful to hear. No good would come from my expressing these asocial instincts — at least not usually.

The writer, however, must loosen the bonds that have held her back all these years. Sexual lust, hate for her own children, the desire to taste the blood of her enemy — all these things and many more must, at times, crowd the writer's mind.

Your protagonist, for instance, may at a certain moment despise his mother. "She stinks of red wine and urine," he thinks. "And she looks like a shriveled, pitted prune."

This is an unpleasant sentiment, to be sure. But does it

bring your hero's character into focus? This is the only question that's important. And there's no getting around it. Your characters will have ugly sides to them; they will be, at times, sexually deviant, bitter, racist, cruel.

"Sure," you say, "the antagonists, the bad guys in my book, will be like that but not the heroes and heroines."

Not so.

The story you tell, the characters you present, will all have dark sides to them. If you want to write believable fiction, you will have to cross over the line of your self-restraint and revel in the words and ideas that you would never express in your everyday life.

Our social moorings aren't the only things that restrain our creative impulses. We are also limited by false aesthetics: those notions that we have developed in schools and libraries, and from listening to critics that adhere to some misplaced notion of a literary canon. Many writers come to the discipline after having read the old, and new, masters. They read Dickens and Melville, Shakespeare and Homer. From these great books of yore, they develop tics and reflexes that cause their words to become stiff and unnatural.

Many writers, and teachers of writing, spend so much time comparing work to past masters that they lose the contemporary voice of the novel being created on this day.

You will not become a writer by aping the tones and phrases, form and content, of great books of the past. Your novel lies in your heart; it is a book about today, no matter in which era it is set, written for a contemporary audience to express a story that could only have come from you.

Don't get me wrong—you can read anything and learn from it. But your learning will also come from modern songs, newscasts, magazine articles, and conversations overheard on the street. A novel is a pedestrian work about the everyday lives of bricklayers and saints.

Another source of restraint for the writer is the use of personal confession and the subsequent guilt that often arises from it. Many writers use themselves, their families, and their friends as models for the characters they portray. A young woman who has had a difficult time with her mother may render a tale in which the mother seems overly harsh, maybe even heartless. She (the writer) wades in, telling the story in all its truth and ugliness, but then, feeling guilt, she backs away from it, muddying the water. Maybe she stops writing for a while or changes her subject.

Whatever it is she does, the novel suffers.

This would-be novelist has betrayed herself in order that she not tell the story that has been clawing its way out from her core. She would rather not commit herself to the truth that she has found in the rigor of writing every day.

This form of restraint is common and wholly unnecessary.

To begin with, your mother is not reading what you have

written. These words are your private preserve until the day they're published.

Also you should wait until the book is finished before making a judgment on its content. By the time you have gone through twenty drafts, the characters may have developed lives of their own, completely separate from the people you based them on in the beginning. And even if someone, at some time, gets upset with your words — so what? Live your life, sing your song. Anyone who loves you will want you to have that.

Don't let any feeling keep you from writing. Don't let the world slow you down. Your story is the most important thing coming down the line this year. It's your year — make the most of it.

avoidance, false starts, and dead-end thinking

Many writers-in-waiting spend a lot of time avoiding the work at hand. The most common way to avoid writing is by procrastination. This is the writer's greatest enemy. There is little to say about it except that once you decide to write every day, you must make yourself sit at the desk or table for the required period whether or not you are putting down words. Make yourself take the time even if the hours seem fruitless. Ideally, after a few days or weeks of being chained to the desk, you will submit to the story that must be told.

Straightforward procrastination is an author's worst enemy, but there are others: the writer who suddenly has chores that have gone undone for months but that now seem urgent; the diarist who develops a keen wish to write about her experiences today instead of writing her book; the Good Samaritan who realizes that there's a world out there that needs saving; the jack-of-all-trades who, when he begins one project, imagines ten others that are equally or even more important.

Forget all that. Don't write in the journal unless you're writing a chapter of your book. Save the world at 8:30 instead of 7:00. Let the lawn get shaggy and the paint peel from the walls.

For that time you have set aside to write your novel, don't do anything else. Turn the ringer off on your phone. Don't answer the doorbell. Tell your loved ones that you cannot be disturbed. And if they cannot bear to live without you, go write in a coffee shop or library. Rent a room if you have to — just make the time to write your book.

a final note about process

The process of writing a novel is like taking a journey by boat. You have to continually set yourself on course. If you get distracted or allow yourself to drift, you will never make it to the destination. It's not like highly defined train tracks or a highway; this is a path that you are creating, discovering. The journey is your narrative. Keep to it and there will be a tale told.

2

The Elements of Fiction

the narrative voice

The voice that tells the story is the first thing the reader encounters. It carries us from the first page to the last. We, the readers, must believe in this narrative voice or, at least, we must feel strongly for that voice and have a definite and consistent opinion about it.

The first words and all the rest you encounter throughout the novel give information, images, and emotions all at once, much the way it happens on that street corner with the guy telling tales.

"Man come outta that burnin' buildin'," Joe Feller said, his voice straining and hoarse, *"red as a lobster with smoke comin' out of his clothes."*

This brief snippet of dialogue brings us immediately into an event that we know some things about while suspecting others. There was a building on fire, we are told. There's a man who was in the fire for some reason. Maybe he was a victim or a hero. It is even possible that he set the fire—we don't know. But Joe Feller's voice has authority, and we're ready to hear him out in order to find out more about this smoking red man.

This is narrative voice. Actually it is more than one voice. There's the character (Joe Feller) speaking, but there's another voice (the narrator) telling us what the speaker said and explaining the speaker's emotional state by describing the strain in his voice.

There are many kinds and styles of narrative voices, and it is imperative that you decide which one you will use to tell your tale. Although there might be thousands of subtle differences in the narratives of the novels you've read, there are only three types that you need to be aware of. Actually there are four, but the last one is a voice you should never use: your own.

first-person narrative

The first-person narrative, put simply, is when the "I" voice is telling the story.

> *I met Josh Sanders on the first day of March 1963. He was a shy man with big hands and an earthy smell about him. He reminded me of my grandfather, whom I hated more than Judas.*

We know from the first word that we have an intimate relationship with the narrator of this tale. He, or she, has a name, an age, and a history that we will learn about as we read. This narrator is our conduit to the novel. She might be a college graduate or an illiterate. She may be enchanting, cantankerous, or even untrustworthy. Every bit of information we learn about this narrator helps us understand more of the story being told.

This is the most familiar storytelling voice, the one with which we all naturally relate the stories of our days to those we know. In a first-person narrative, you are stuck with this one voice. Therefore this character, or at least her *point of view (POV)*, must be engaging. Her story must evoke strong feelings in us. We are compelled to empathize with her experiences and care about the world she moves through. We have an emotional connection to this narrator, and because of this bond, we want to learn what happens in her story.

Not that every iota of information in the novel must come directly from that voice. Your narrator, let's call her Sally, will meet people along the way, talk to them, overhear their conversations; she will read letters and newspaper articles; she will have dreams in which important events in her life may be revealed. You could even have Sally read parts of another novel or work of nonfiction that have a completely different narrative voice. There are dozens of ways to break up the narrative even in the first person. But everything flows through the consciousness of this narrator, so you must be true to that voice.

When I say that you must be true to this narrator's voice, I mean, among other things, that you can't change her personality to fit the story. She cannot read the minds of other characters; she can know only what she has experienced or learned. And she is limited by her circumstances (e.g., her physical location at any given moment, her education, her situation in life, her emotional state, etc.).

The first-person narrator is the doorway through which all the information of this story will pass; therefore the sense the reader has of this character must never be challenged. You can never undercut her authority. You cannot, for instance, insert a phrase such as "Sally never knew her mother because Nelda Smith had died in childbirth." Who said that? Not Sally, of course. The writer said it. The writer's voice has intruded into the story. This will destroy the reader's faith in the words he or she is reading. The novel careens out of orbit and the story is lost. If you need to convey specific information, Sally must either think it, say it, read it, remember it, or hear someone else talking about it.

This example is extreme, but the writer can make other more subtle and yet equally disastrous intrusions.

Your main character, let's say, is not very well educated. We know this because of her limited vocabulary, her simple sentence structures, and hints that have been dropped along the way. But somewhere someone asks her a question, to which she answers, "Indubitably, my good sir." Say what? Who said that? The writer, not the character.

Or perhaps your narrator all of a sudden understands something behind another person's actions in a way that strains the credulity of the reader. For the whole story up to this point, Sally hasn't understood anything psychological, but suddenly she thinks, "He seemed to have issues with his mother. I could tell this because he would never look women directly in the eye." This is perfectly fine to say if the reader believes from the book so far that Sally has this kind of insight into psychological motivations. But if she has not given any indication of having this sort of sensitivity in the first two hundred pages, and then magically manifests this ability, the reader will become confused and the story will miscarry.*

The first-person narrative is a powerful but also very difficult narrative form. It is powerful because you are intimate with the emotions and internal processes of the very real human being telling you the story; it is difficult because the rendering of that character has to be pitch-perfect for the reader to believe in her.

There is also the difficulty of making sure that the first-person narrator is interesting enough to want to listen to for hundreds of pages.

---

*Part of this issue has to do with character development within the story. We'll get to that later on.

third-person narrative

The third-person narrator is the voice in which we naturally tell stories about things that happened to people other than ourselves. This narrative voice is not a full person. Picture the third-person narrator as a small, emotionless, but intelligent creature sitting on the shoulder of the character who is experiencing the story. This creature perceives events from the perspective of this character and every now and then has glimmers of what this character might be feeling or thinking.

> *Brent Farley entered the room, looking around for his mother.*
> *Instead he saw Alice Norman standing near the buffet. She noticed him and smiled before he had the opportunity to flee.*
> *"Hello, Alice," Brent said, holding out his hand.*
> *Her fingers were cold, and so, Brent noticed, were her eyes.*

As with the first-person narrative, we are entering the story through the experiences of an individual. But in this case we aren't so intimate with all the nuances of his character. Instead we are viewing the world through the prism of the intelligent eye perched on Brent's shoulder, an intelligence without emotional response. It is important that the third-person narrator have a distance from the passions of the novel's character. If you begin to give this narrative voice a personality, it can confuse the reader, giving them the feeling that they are being told how to feel about and see this world rather than spying on it from behind a one-way mirror.

The cooler third-person narrator allows us to see the world of this novel from a certain impartial remove. This gives a kind of balance to the fiction that permits a reader to more easily suspend their disbelief.

This, I believe, is a steadier voice than the first-person POV. You are given information by an even-tempered voice, which is good. At the same time, in this voice it can be harder to bring out the emotional depth of your characters than in the first person. You can give momentary glimpses into the mind of the shoulder you're on, but you cannot, as a rule, get deeply into their heart.

One benefit of this form of narrative is that the dispassionate observer can, at times, leap from the shoulder of one character onto that of another.

Let us suppose that the meeting between Brent and Alice did not go very well. At the end of that chapter or section, Brent is left wondering if she suspects him of mishandling her affairs.

At the beginning of the next scene, we find our narrative eye on the shoulder of Alice as she walks down the street in the long, darkening shadows of buildings her family once owned. She meets an old friend, who tells her to watch out for Brent — he's not in any way a trustworthy man and would take the rest of her dwindling fortune if he could.

"I just ran into him," Alice said. "He seemed to want to get away from me as soon as possible. As a matter of fact, when I first saw him he was looking my way and I swear I thought he was about to bolt through the door."

Nareen Padam's eyes got tight, giving her a contemplative air, as if Alice had posed a riddle.

"Maybe," dark-eyed Nareen said, "he was worried that you'd figured out one of his schemes against you and your family. Maybe he was afraid you'd make a scene."

After this meeting, your narrator could jump to Nareen's shoulder, but I wouldn't suggest it. The third-person narrator should be picky about the experiences it uses to tell the story.

This form of narration can utilize the POVs of one, two, three, or more characters, but there has to be a reason for each narrative to exist. If your story is formed around a conflict, you should use a POV from each side of that discord. If the novel is about a corporate takeover, you might need eight or nine voices to cover all the subtle sides of the tale.

It is possible to use only one POV to tell your story. Why, you ask, would I use the third-person narrative for only one voice? Why wouldn't I just use the first-person narrative instead? There might be many valid reasons for this decision. For instance, your character may be a cipher to himself. He's not a reflective type who goes about articulating what he sees and feels. Or conversely, he might be too expressive and flamboyant and in need of the cool reserve of a slightly removed POV.

Narrative voice is a subtle thing. You have to decide what voice fits your task. But I will tell you that the third-person narrative will probably best serve your first novel—the one you are writing this year. This form is the most flexible and durable.

One more thing you should know about this form:

As I have said, the third-person narrator has *some* of the knowledge of the shoulder he's on. So when Alice sees Nareen, the narrative voice might be aware of the fondness Alice has for this young woman and might even possess some additional specific knowledge.

> *Alice ran into Nareen turning the corner at Third and Barton Streets. A feeling of familiar warmth came over her when she saw her old friend. Alice observed that the dark-skinned young woman maintained only the broad facial features of her mother's Swedish stock. Everything else was inherited from her father, whom Alice had heard was a criminal lawyer from Bombay who migrated to Michigan because his Scandinavian bride wanted him to meet her halfway.*

the omniscient narrator

The omniscient narrator is the most powerful and most difficult narrative form. The omniscient narrator knows all. He could tell you the story about Brent and Alice and Nareen, but if he wanted to he could also tell you about what is going on at that moment in Cuba or relate the dialogue between fleas on a rat's back beneath the street where Nareen and Alice are talking. The omniscient narrator doesn't need any one person or some emotionless eye on the shoulder to tell the story. It is the all-seeing eye of God.

> *Brent Farley walked into the room looking for his mother, but instead he found Alice Norman standing near the buffet.*
>
> *Alice noted that Brent seemed uneasy. "It's almost as if he wants to get away from me," she thought.*
>
> *"She's looking at me," Brent reflected, thinking that the red color in her dress was meant for a younger woman.*
>
> *Lawrence Smith-Jones, the club maître d', noticed the two and remembered them as children running madly in mud-spattered jeans down near the stream behind the club.*

This voice is a potent one. Nothing that happens is beyond its reach. The omniscient narrator can cure cancer, explain what the meaning of life truly is, travel through space and time with impossible ease.

The promise of such power is seductive, but it contains hidden dangers for the first-time novelist. The main problem is the reader: Can you convince him that you are all-knowing? Can your narrative maintain the tension between characters while at the same time speaking with such clarity and superior knowledge?

The reader approaches the novel as a story that has to unfold in a certain unique fashion. She doesn't know where the tale is going. She doesn't know if Brent is really a bad man who is intent on beggaring Alice and her family.

In the first-person narrative from Brent's POV, Brent would know his own intentions, but he wouldn't know the content of Alice's heart and certainly would not be privy to the conversation between Nareen and Alice.

The third-person narrator has no deep knowledge of any of the characters, so we have to rely on dramatic interaction to unearth the truth.

But the omniscient narrator knows all. If he doesn't tell us something, it is because he decides to withhold that information. If he does tell us, it is absolute truth with no gradations of gray. The omniscient narrative voice therefore runs the risk of killing the dramatic tension you are trying to create.

This is not to say that one should never use this voice. Many, many novels (especially those written in the nineteenth century and earlier) use this voice magnificently.

The proper omniscient narrator's voice can be used effectively with the understanding that even the voice of God can have slight variations and rules by which it decides to impart information.

For instance, your omniscient narrator might be so high and mighty that she doesn't waste time wondering about the truths or complex motivations of the characters she presents.

Captain Jack Hatter was a seafaring man who got it in mind that he was in love with a princess. He gathered a company of rough-and-ready tars who were willing to follow the handsome young officer to the ends of the earth — as long as there was plunder now and then along the way. . . .

Princess Jasmine Alonza Trevor-MacFord was aware of Hatter's passion, but she never let on if she would be a willing partner to his lust. When her girl-servants talked about Hatter's promise to take her by force from her father's lands, Jasmine would smile mysteriously and change the subject to the weather. . . .

From this POV the omniscient narrator *could* tell us many things about her characters but prefers not to. The storytelling is held at a certain distance to keep the reader wondering on many levels: Will Jack take the princess? Will the princess welcome his advances?

This is just one of many possible approaches an omniscient narrative might take. This voice spends most of its time disguised as a third-person narrator but appears in its full force often enough to let us know that there is more to it. Or, the omniscient narrator may place limits upon itself by letting information come out only in a certain time sequence or by individuals giving voice to their feelings.

There are many ways to spin the omniscient narrator so that the unfolding of the novel is still a wonder to the reader.

The problem is that this voice of God has to learn how to limit itself, whereas the first- and third-person narrative voices have built-in limits.

final notes on narrative voice

First- and third-person narrative voices bring with them limitations on what the characters in the novel can say and know.

The first-person narrative can know only what the speaker knows. This tale is limited by the mind and senses, the situation and sophistication, the gender and education, of the narrator.

The third-person narrator benefits from different POVs but can portray only one of these at a time, and there is the further limit that this dispassionate POV cannot, most of the time, delve too deeply into any one character's inner workings.

These limitations may seem difficult and overly exacting, but I believe that they are the best thing for the first-time novelist. The restrictions placed on the prose by these rules are stringent, but they are also organic in the storytelling sense. That is to say, we live third- and first-person lives.

Personally we know what it is we think and feel. We pass through this life making silent comments on events going on around us. Sometimes we interact with people with conspicuous honesty; other times, not so much. We feel love and hate and fear, and so does everyone else in the world. The fact that everyone knows life primarily through personal experience means that, if a first-person narrative is executed scrupulously, the reader will naturally identify with the voice.

Similarly we all have some experience with the third-person narrative. We have jobs in which people are continually talking: talking to each other, talking behind each other's back, seducing, expounding, bragging, lying. We are often silent witnesses to encounters on the bus, on the street, or maybe even through apartment walls. We all know what it is to be a silent observer, so when presented with the experience of cool remove that the third-person narrator perfects, we feel that we can understand the story — or at least we are given an opportunity to understand.

The omniscient narrator is a little larger than what we're used to. This form has no limitations that are not self-imposed. This does not mean that you cannot write a novel from this voice. The problem is that you have to be a consummate storyteller with extraordinary self-control to tell a story in this way.

Other voices are possible. Novels have been written entirely in the first-person *plural,* told entirely by an unspecified *we.* Others address the reader as "you" throughout. But these are idiosyncratic and challenging approaches to storytelling. My advice is that you use the third-person narrative to write your novel (this year). But of course you will do as your heart tells you to.

showing and telling

"The words came right up off the page." This is the highest possible praise for the fiction writer. It means that when reading the book, the reader felt that they were actually experienc-ing the sensations and emotions, the life and atmosphere, depicted by the novelist.

The accomplished writer achieves this level of realism by using language that is active and metaphorical, economically emotional yet also pedestrian.

As often as possible the fiction writer shows us events and active characters, vivid images and real dialogue, rather than telling us about the inner workings of someone's mind or the *reality* of a situation.

> *Lance Piggott had a great bulbous face, with black pinpoints for eyes and pasty white skin. He spoke in short bursts like a semi-automatic weapon. The bloated leather of his shoes seemed about to burst open from the pressure of his bulging feet. Monsieur Piggott was indeed an explosion about to happen. His secretary, VernaMae Warren, would lean away from him whenever he approached her desk or stomped up to her side when she was pulling files from the green metal cabinets. The skittish secretary feared she would be obliterated by the mere proximity of her juggernaut of a boss.*

This in-depth description supplants the more cogent

> *Lance Piggott was a large, violent man. His secretary, Verna-Mae Warren, avoided him whenever possible.*

It is often better if you use images and physical descrip-tions rather than mere informative language to present people, places, things, and events in your novel. To be told that someone is violent or seems to be violent is too general; the reader is left to come up with their own notions of Piggott based upon their personal experience with violence. But to describe a man who, at every moment, is about to explode helps the reader have a specific sense of that character.

The strong scent of pine tar and eucalyptus stung Mary's nostrils. The woodlands were alive with the racket of life. Insects clicked and buzzed; what must have been a bird gave a strangled cry, while somewhere a creature, hidden by the dense green-and-gray forest, crunched away, causing the young woman to imagine an ogre gnawing on a tree trunk.

All the while the sun seared her skin. Mary felt a deep satisfaction with the lancing pain and dissonant woodland sounds. It was as if, she thought, she were a wild thing set loose in an unremitting Eden.

This attempt to present your protagonist's experience of a wildwood area works better than

The sun-beaten woods were rank smelling, filled with dissonant sounds. Oddly, Mary felt at home there.

I hope that these examples begin to illustrate the difference between showing and telling in fiction.

To simply say that Lance Piggott is a violent man is less

persuasive than portraying him as a time bomb loose on the world.

Of course a character that is violent, or seems so, might not have the physical attributes or traits that describe his or her nature. Your character, let's call her Fawn, might be petite and sweet-looking. In this case you could choose the actions she takes when she's alone to describe her. She could torture small animals or imagine tormenting and killing a rival; she could, talking sweetly but breathing hard, tell a friend that she would beat in her head with a baseball bat if that friend ever crossed her.

A character talking is an action too.

I know that there are the sticklers out there among you who will say that everything expressed in words is told, not shown. After all, telling is a function of speaking, and writing is nothing but an extension of speech. This is true. But there's a difference between explanation and verbal action.

For instance, "Call me Ishmael" is the well-known first line of the American classic *Moby Dick*. Contrast this sentence with "His name was Ishmael."

What's the difference between the two beginnings? The first is definitely stronger on its own. But why? I believe that it is because the original introduction is active; it invites the reader into conversation with a character who, the reader feels, intends to stay around for a while. The character is going to introduce the reader to his world.

"His name was Ishmael" is a flat statement that does not, on its own, draw us in. It is merely a piece of information.

The first example shows something to the reader, or, more accurately, *it attempts to include the reader by engaging with him on a personal level.* In this case, Ishmael is conversing with us. In the first example concerning Mary, she not only smells the forest, but the pine tar and eucalyptus burn her nostrils. This is something else that the reader can imagine feeling.

So I suppose the clearest difference between telling and showing in fiction is, generally, the difference between a purely informational statement and one that attempts to add a human aspect to its repertoire and, in doing so, includes the reader either emotionally or physically.

There are many ways to *show* in language. Below you will find a few of them.

sensations

When experiencing life, we often have physical sensations. Our tongues go dry, the hair stands up on the backs of our necks, our eyelids start twitching. Some people become flatulent when they're afraid. If you can include the physical reactions to the emotional situations that your characters find themselves in, you will be bringing your readers closer to the experience of the novel.

If the sensation is one that seems out of place, the reader will want to understand, will want to know more. For instance, a police officer in the execution of his duty is restraining a woman who is trying to stop his partner from arresting her husband. In the struggle with the screaming, clawing woman, the restraining officer experiences an erection. You could say that he experienced sexual arousal — you might decide that this is the best way to put it. Readers will certainly wonder what's going on with that cop.

emotions

Gazing into her walnut-colored eyes, he saw a speck that reminded him of that island he dreamed of as a boy, that place he'd always yearned to be. . . .

I know, maybe a little sappy, but you see where I'm going.

Emotions inform our responses to the physical world, and our language reflects those responses: I saw red; her heart skipped a beat; I turned to jelly; my blood ran cold. These are all common phrases used to express what we feel in our bodies. To say "I love you," or "I love him [or her or it]," rather than using a more vivid expression is not strong enough for fiction. You have to get down to the place where the character (and therefore the reader) feels the emotions that drive your novel.

Maybe your main character as a rule experiences the world as loud sounds and sharp edges. He winces when his boss speaks; he feels the rims of his shoes biting into his ankles when he walks. But when he goes to lunch with Marianne, all of a sudden things become soft and rounded — the air, which burned his lungs on the street, is now soothing him, restoring him. His feet have stopped hurting, and the music being played in the background transports him to a sylvan childhood scene.

Making emotions physical or imagistic helps bring your reader more deeply into the story. Of course you will have to have many simple informative sentences about the characters' feelings throughout the text, but you must question every time you use flat descriptive language to describe an emotion, impression, or realization.

the pedestrian in fiction

Maybe your main character gets up out of bed and walks across the room to the mirror. You need her to see the bags under her eyes and lines on her aging face. That's good. But in order to have us feel what it is to get up out of that bed, we might want to add a little more: the sound of the sheets falling to the floor; the urge to urinate, which the protagonist resists in order to see what time and life have wrought upon her visage; the grit beneath her bare feet on the floor; the pain in her left knee that has been with her since a time, years ago, when she twisted her ankle on a stone stairway while attending her mother's funeral — the mother whom she now so very much resembles. Every one of these details tells and also shows us something about our protagonist and/or her world.

Most of the details are pedestrian. Why, you might ask, would we want to make the experiences of our character ordinary? Because everyday experiences help the reader relate to the character, which sets up the reader's acceptance of more extraordinary events that may unfold.

If your audience believes in the daily humdrum physical and emotional experiences of your characters, then your readers will believe in those characters' reality and thus can be taken further.

metaphor and simile

Lemon Turner was a lion among sheep. Whenever he entered a room, men and women shied away, huddling together behind tables and glancing nervously toward the exits.

The above example uses metaphor. Lemon Turner is not lion-*like*—he *is* a lion; the people around him do not *resemble* sheep—they *are* sheep. Lemon's mere presence turns human beings into herd animals that bleat and run.

The metaphor is the strongest imagistic intimation in the writer's bag of tricks.

Haystack Olds was a brick wall, while Mike Minter might as well have been made from straw. You got the feeling that every punch Mike threw hurt him more than it did Haystack.

Tyne was a clean, clear northern wind blowing away the detritus of Charles's messy home.

The metaphor helps broaden the appreciation of the reader. When, later in Lemon's tale, a young woman comes up to him holding her head in such a way that she bares her throat, we achieve an added feeling of tension because we know Lemon's nature. When an unruly child comes into Tyne's space, we wonder if he will be blown away or sat up straight.

The metaphor definitely shows us something — something that we both see and imagine. Tyne cannot look like an invisible gale, but her wake and her energy remind us of an open window on a gusty day. Lemon might not have a great mane of hair, but the reader's imagination will imbue him with a feral voice or lithe step.

And it's not only human beings that are transformed by metaphor; anything in the writer's realm can also be something else.

The sun, for instance, can be a grueling taskmaster who, with solar whip in hand, drives your characters across the vast plain of your novel.

Once you set a metaphor in a reader's mind, it will stay with them for many pages. It will free their imaginations and help you with the telling of your tale.

But be careful: you shouldn't overuse this tool. A man who is straw, another who is brick, a lion loose in the house with a woman who is also a wind — all together these could be too much. Overuse of metaphorical language will test a novel's credibility.

You must also be true to the metaphors you use. If a man is a lion, leave him that way. Don't make him into a wall or a wind too. This is called mixing metaphor — a sure way to lose your reader.

Sometimes you need an image, but the full-blown metaphor is too strong. That's okay. We have a tool for the milder image making — the simile.

> *Her skin was like fine china, white and brittle-looking, etched here and there with faded blue images — tattoos that would mark her for life.*

We are not afraid to touch this woman. We know that she actually has human skin — skin that is *reminiscent* of fired clay. We hold the cobalt-glazed-porcelain image in our minds, knowing all the while that if she fell, she would not shatter.

There are all kinds of similes. You could say that her skin was like china, her eyes like angry skies, his fists like stone, or their combined presence and mien was as a stand of great oaks — dignified and somber.

The simile tries our credulity less than the metaphor; it also creates a weaker image.

But the simile allows the reader to see more clearly the

two sides of the subject—that which is its normal state and also the image it is compared to. Sometimes this sort of double vision fits the novelist's purposes more closely than the dynamic metaphor.

Depending on the demands of your story, you may have either similes or metaphors—or both—in your novel (the one you are writing this year). They will enhance the reader's vision of the places and characters you are presenting, and they will show the reader, without lifeless explanations, what that world looks like and how it feels to be there.

final note on showing and telling

What you must always remember is that the novel is more experiential than it is informational. Your reader might learn something, but most of what they learn is gained through what they are shown about the lives and circumstances of the characters therein.

character and character development

All novels, short stories, and plays, and most poems, are about human transformation. The subject of the novel is the human spirit and psyche—how the characters interact in their relationships with other souls and with the world in general. In some stories the human being might be replaced by a metaphor-made-real such as a robot with a soul or a pig with the ability to speak and think—but these simulacra are just another way of looking at ourselves.

In the novel there has to be movement in the personality structure of the main character or characters. This is to say that, in part, the purpose of the novel is to map out the events in the protagonist's life that cause her to change. This change and the events that flow from it are why we read and write books.

And so the characters in the novel must be completely believable. They will have to stand up to the closest scrutiny by readers, editors, and critics. One of the most important things that you will do this year will be to create complex, authentic characters that begin at one point in their lives and advance (or devolve) to another.

The following example is a longish outline of a dramatic arc that will serve to not only elucidate character development but also introduce you to other aspects of writing that we will cover later on in this book. Bear with this story, and I promise that your tolerance will be repaid.

Bob Millar and his family, while traveling through the southwestern desert, are kidnapped by a gang of brigands who brutalize Bob; rape and murder his wife, Amy, and his daughter, Leanne; kill his son Aldo outright; and blind his youngest boy, Lyle. After this first wave of violence, the attackers, under the influence of drugs and alcohol, fall into a stupor. Bob, badly beaten and half blind himself, takes Lyle up in his arms and runs three miles through the desert night.

When he is maybe a mile away from the killers' encampment, he hears a wild cry from their maniacal leader. Bob continues to run, followed by the yells of his pursuers, finally coming to a road, where a passing moving van stops to help him.

The above is the central event of the novel.

I might begin the book with Bob running through the desert, his disoriented son swooning in his arms, asking, almost incoherently, about his mother and siblings. While running, Bob obsessively remembers the drive into the desert and the petty argument he was having with Amy. Underlying this spat was a suspicion that Bob has harbored for years: he has long suspected that Amy and his friend Alfred Jones had an affair.

In this way I get to know Bob at the fundamental moment of his transition. We see the husband and wife taking jabs at each other, and then we hear the bloodcurdling screams in the darkness.

Maybe we also learn that the child, Lyle, loves chocolate.

And there we have it. Bob Millar, with his blind son in his arms, running out of his old life and into a terrible new phase in which he will have to learn many things: He will have to forgive himself for failing to protect his family. He will have to help his son deal with the pain of his losses. Somehow he will have to overcome the terror wrought upon him by the land pirates who decimated so many lives.

Looking at the beginning of a novel in this way, we are confronted with many of the basic elements of fiction writing. There's the story, the plot, the characters, and the serious underlying question—what is the novel about?

But right now all we care about is character and character development, and the only character we will discuss in detail is Bob and his redemption—or his downfall.

Bob is a weak man in many ways. He suspects that his wife had a passionate affair with his friend and even that his youngest son, the blind boy in his arms, may be the fruit of that union. But despite his suspicions, he has remained silent all these years. He has become spiteful and petty. His marriage has turned into a bitter dance in which he and Amy move around each other in a ballet of continual resentment.

After the truck driver takes father and son to the police, Bob collapses. Amy's parents come to collect Lyle. They try to talk to Bob in his hospital bed, but he sees them as if they were very far away. His lips are numb and his voice is strained. He wants them to leave.

When he is told that he's lost the sight in the injured eye, he doesn't seem to care. When he's told that his son will be raised by his in-laws, he says, "He probably wasn't mine anyway." Bob's boss sends his secretary, Ramona, to tell Bob that he's being replaced but will receive unemployment insurance and disability.

Bob's response to his loss of employment is to tell Ramona that they never liked him at work. He seems to have developed a very clear vision of himself—an almost objective POV that allows him to know things that he never was able to understand before. This knowledge, however, is impotent—it does not push him to take action.

"No one has ever really known me," Bob says. "If I was someone else, maybe Brian [his boss] would have found a place for me. I wouldn't have stayed, but . . ."

Failing to lighten Bob's mood, Ramona promises to return. Bob forgets her immediately upon her departure.

For a while Bob wonders about himself. He remembers his children and his wife, the days spent criticizing Amy. These memories might be punctuated with the last moments of each family member's life.

He remembers his mother (Bernadette) and how unhappy she was living with his stepfather, Simon.

There is no solace in Bob's earlier life memories. He has, it seems, always been taciturn and bitter.

The doctor informs Bob that his insurance will not cover any further time in the hospital. While he is dressing to leave, the police come and inform him that they have caught the killers; they need him to come down and identify them. He tries, but the moment they open the curtains to the lineup, he faints. . . .

We now have Bob's character set in our mind. We know who he was before the vicious attack. We know what a wreck he is now. We also see the possible ways he might go. Will he gain the courage to face his attackers? Will he forgive Amy? Will he and Ramona have something more than he'd known before? Will he find out that Lyle is not his son and love him anyway?

What will become of Bob? Who will emerge from the novel?

These last two questions are difficult. They represent the structure of Bob's character-to-be. It doesn't matter how the author treats him. Maybe Bob sinks into a malaise and dies unredeemed. Maybe his son rises as the hero of the book. Maybe Bob smuggles a gun into the trial and kills the (so far) nameless psycho that murdered his family.

Maybe he forgives the killers.

What matters is that you hook the readers on Bob's predicament (in this case, a crisis) and make them intimate with his limitations and the issues he has to resolve in order to overcome the impediments in his path. There is no novel unless Bob experiences a transition. And there can be no meaningful transition unless we feel deeply for Bob.

And it's not only Bob. Every character we meet in this year's novel must have something uniquely human about them — the waitress (who appears only on one page of the book) with the remnants of a shiner about her left eye; the killer who regrets his acts; the wife who, in Bob's memory, holds on fiercely to her independence and the value of her life.

Lyle, Bob's sole surviving child, must come to grips with his blindness and his father's abandonment. Ramona has to have a reason to want to help Bob. This means that she has a history that we must at least partially uncover in order to understand her motivations.

Most novels follow various central characters to differing degrees. Each of these people must have a definite nature that engages the reader's attention.

A character is made up of many attributes: the way he talks; her age and education; his level of cleanliness; his bravery or cowardice; their love of life or sex or food.

As with the metaphor, you should not give your character too many traits or tics. You must choose those attributes, features, characteristics, or qualities that help to define this character—to make him memorable and, to some degree, predictable.

But beyond revealing the shallow traits that help the reader know the players in your tale, you must make the characters express those deep feelings that will allow us to anticipate (with fear and joy) their transition.

As in life, your characters develop mainly because of their dealings with one another. The complex and dynamic interplay of relationships throughout the course of the novel is what makes change possible.

One of the primary ways we learn is through our relationships with other human beings. But what we learn is not always accurate or good. We might decide from watching our parents that women exist to serve men. We might decide that the foreigners down the street are unworthy of trust, incapable of love.

The mistakes we make in life are what make us interesting. The errors your characters make, more than any other thing, will drive the engrossing aspects of your novel.

a final note on character development

Not all characters face the extreme dramatic tension that Bob Millar experienced. Any change in a character can be the subject of a novel—a young girl's conflict with her stepmother has repercussions across an extended family; a man opening to love with a pet begins to see a world he never suspected; a student decides to become an artist even though her parents want her to be a doctor, she thinks.

There is always conflict in character development, but this can be a subtle divergence.

George decides to take a different route on his walk to work.
This new path shows him three things: a pastry shop, a magic store,
and an old man who stands on a corner selling books. These ele-

ments become central to George's beginning to understand that he has wasted his life.

story

A man loses his magic goose. He looks all over the country-side, trying to find his beloved pet. This adventure takes him far from home. Somewhere on the journey the man realizes that he loved his pet but neglected her. He almost gives up hope, but then, in the barn next to his home, he finds the goose sleeping on a bed of hay.

This, in its basic form, is a story.

A story doesn't have to be elaborate, convoluted, or hard to explain. The most elegant story lines are often simple and straightforward: an aging man, losing his memory to old age, tries to retain what is important; girl meets boy, girl loses boy, girl realizes that she just missed a disaster; a couple climb a mountain to pay homage to their son, who died courageously and alone — along the way they find that they've lost each other.

A story is a simple thing. It is a narrative that has a beginning, middle, and end.

A man, we'll call him Trip, tells his wife, Marissa, that while he was out taking a walk, he ran into an old friend. This friend invited Trip to a bar, where the friend plied him with a sugary concoction that didn't at all taste like it was one-third gin. When the police got there, Trip had no idea that the girls (his friend's friends) at their table were underage. . . .

Stories are often lies. More often, they are only partial truths.

What makes a story interesting? A subject that is absorbing and the way in which that story is told. A guy who hangs out around the watercooler at work engages you by using not only the power of the story but also his gestures and his voice. He winks, bellows, and grins knowingly while telling the story his friend told his wife after getting arrested at a bar known for prostitution. The storyteller has you doubled over with laughter. He relates the yarn word for word, just the way Trip must have done when explaining to his wife about his travails. But the tone of the storyteller's voice and the delivery allow you to perceive a completely different meaning on top of Trip's explanations.

As a novelist I have often wished that I could tell my stories to each and every one of my readers and critics. "If only I could explain to them exactly what this phrase means," I think. But this is not possible. The oral storyteller has me beat. He has a whole repertoire of physical tools not available in print. So when I'm telling a story, I have to re-create the winks and nods, insinuations and emotional outbursts, with words alone. I have to create a world for the reader that is just as intimate as that watercooler setting.

So maybe I have Trip's wife, Marissa, coming to her

mother's house to ask for the money to pay Trip's fine. This will be a larger story, designed to contain the more humorous one of Trip's great adventure.

Marissa's mother is a forty-year-old woman, named Love by her hippie parents. She is dour and untrusting. She hates Trip and thinks that her daughter is an idiot. Marissa believes Trip's story—why wouldn't she? After all, Victor, the friend who got Trip into trouble, didn't tell Trip about the girls. He really didn't know. . . .

The first story, Marissa and Love's conversation, is the water-cooler. Here we are told, at the same time Love is, about the dubious tale that Trip unloaded on his wife. We see the complex relationship between Marissa and Love. We may take sides with one or the other.

As an introduction to the novel, this brings deeper levels of interest than the everyday oral tale. We are introduced to a much larger story than Trip's perfidy or innocence.

At the end of this first scene or chapter, Love either helps Marissa or doesn't. Trip is sent to jail (this is his third offense, let's say) or he comes home.

We laugh about Trip's adventure but feel sorry for Marissa. Why doesn't she see that this man is no good for her? Why doesn't Love see the trusting beauty of her daughter's heart? Why is Trip such a fool?

*   *   *

A novel is both a larger story and an accumulation of many smaller stories, such as the ones about Love and Marissa, and Trip at the bar.

intuition versus structure

At this point we have to ask the question—what is the larger story, or what is the novel about? For some writers, the intuitive kind, this might be a very difficult question to answer at first. They started writing the tale because of a story they heard at work about a guy somewhat like Trip. In their re-creation of the tale, they came up with Marissa, a girl much like Janey Fine, whom they knew in high school. Love, the mother, is their aunt from Spokane. This chapter was just a way to get into the larger story, whatever that might be.

For the intuitive writer, there is no necessity to know the overall subject of *Trip's Night in Jail*. From here they might have to slog through writing hundreds of pages before the larger story makes any sense to them.

But the structured writer, the kind that knows from the first word that they are telling Marissa's story of self-realization and ultimate liberation, will have a much different approach to the text.

For this writer the next scene or chapter will take Marissa to a predestined place. For the sake of argument, we'll say Marissa goes to the county jail to see Trip and tell him that her mother has refused to post his bail. Love wants Trip in jail and Marissa to move back home.

The structured writer knows her story from beginning to end before she sets pen to paper. If you ask her if Trip and Marissa stay together in the end, she will reply without the slightest hesitation. She knows every beat of Marissa's story.

The intuitive and structured methods are equally valid. Whether you start out knowing the whole story or you don't know a thing beyond the opening scene, you will still have a finished novel at the end of your labors.

This end product is worth a bit of discussion.

The structured writer knows from the outset that the novel is about Marissa, that Trip and Love, and people like them, are two sides of the same impediment that has always kept Marissa from flowering into a realized person (whatever that means). The act of writing is just finding the right way to tell the story. I mean, even an accomplished watercooler orator must tell his story in such a way that the listener will be entertained. The oral storyteller might practice his tale a dozen times on as many individuals before he gets just the right delivery.

The intuitive writer, on the other hand, must *discover* the subject of his story. He follows Marissa from Love's ranch-style house to the jailhouse to Victor's apartment—where she's running an errand for the imprisoned Trip. In this way the writer slowly gets to know his subject. The more he writes (and rewrites), the clearer this story becomes.

This instinctive method of writing is random in appearance, but that is not to say that it is less ordered. Discovering knowledge from your well of unconscious information looks sloppy, but we must always remember that there are no straight lines in the chaos of our hidden minds.

Whether your approach is structured or intuitive, you will have to discover form in your novel. As I said before, the novel is an accumulation of many stories coming together to tell a larger tale. Each of these stories (e.g., Trip's adventure at the bar) will have a beginning, middle, and end; they will also lead into another part of the novel (in this case, Marissa going to her mother for help). The first section of this proposed novel will contain two stories that happen simultaneously: (1) What happened to Trip, and (2) Marissa coming to her mother and telling her the story about Trip.

The intuitive writer, out of the practice of writing each day, will come upon these stories as they occur. Maybe this writer will decide to separate Trip's adventure from the mother-daughter tale; maybe she will start out with Marissa going to the jail and telling Trip what her mother said and did.

The structured writer may break down the whole novel into brief numbered descriptions of each story, chapter, or section. For example:

1) Marissa goes to see her mother after finding out about her husband's arrest.

2) Marissa goes back to Trip, telling him that she can't raise bail. He wheedles her into raiding her college fund.

3) Marissa goes to the bank and lies to the manager, who is a friend of Love's. The manager stalls her, promising to have a check by morning.

4) Victor comes to Marissa's home and offers to help, seducing her with his promises.

5) Love comes to Marissa's when she finds out from the bank manager about Marissa's request. There, she finds Victor in Trip's housecoat. . . .

This outline either will come before you write the novel (i.e., the structured approach) or will be implied after you've finished (i.e., the intuitive way).

Most writers are not entirely intuitive or structured. Most of us have parts of both in our approach to fiction. Maybe we know the beginning and end of our story in general terms, but that's all. Maybe we know every beat of the tale, but in the telling we change key moments. It doesn't matter if you change your approach when writing your book. It is the novel that matters, not the literary religion of the writer.

engagement

The story's job is to engage the reader. She, the reader, becomes concerned about Marissa and at the same time sympathizes with Love's point of view. The reader has a good friend who once had a boyfriend like Trip. The way the writer explains the desert community in which they all live exposes the beauty and ignorance of semirural life in the contemporary Southwest, or at least the reader is persuaded to believe in that ignorance and beauty.

The reader wants to know more about these characters and their humorous and sometimes poignant predicaments. From the moment that Love looks at Marissa's chipped red nails and says, "Either put the nail polish on or take it off," and Marissa replies, "Yes, Mama," putting her hands in her jeans pockets, we know that these people have a story to their lives.

The author pulls out all the stops, regaling us with language and characters and descriptions that pique our interest.

This is the hook — the hook you use to catch readers, not the one that is used to pull the bad actor offstage.

And, to continue the metaphor, once you've hooked the reader, you have to work them until they are reeled in and on the deck. Throughout the novel, you will have to keep up their interest in the characters they've met and the ones they are yet to meet. You have to show them more interesting sides of this community, and they will have to feel even more about Marissa and Trip and Love.

For the entire novel, you will have to keep them wanting to know more and wanting to know what will come of it all. Mastering plot will achieve these ends for you.

plot

To keep your audience reading, you have to make them wonder—after each action, chapter, or scene—what happens next? Will Love dominate her daughter's marriage? Will Marissa see that Trip is lying? What will happen if Marissa goes up to Victor's apartment in the middle of the night? I need to know. I have to turn the page.

So . . . you don't, when you introduce Victor, say, "Trip's friend Victor, who will later seduce Marissa when she comes to his apartment to borrow bail money to get Trip out of jail . . ."

You let the reader worry that Marissa may be set upon by this sexual predator, but you don't let them know what will happen. We already know that Victor is a hound from Trip's story about the bar. We also know that Marissa is an innocent, and we are worried about what Victor might do.

By holding back essential information, we arouse the reader's curiosity and keep them reading; this is the function of plot.

Plot is the structure of revelation—that is to say, it is the method and timing with which you impart important details of the story so that the reader will know just enough to be engaged while still wanting to know more.

So, for instance, in the previous example of Bob Millar running from his torturers, I mentioned that we might learn that his son Lyle loves chocolate. At the time we get this detail, we believe that it is just a bit of character explication for the suffering boy. Indeed, this is true. But later Bob realizes that his son has sunk into depression because of his blindness and that no one can seem to reach him. Bob brings Lyle to their house and puts him in the center of his old room. He tells Lyle that he has put secret caches of the boy's favorite chocolates in hiding places around the room. If Lyle wants to find those delicacies, he has to come down to Bob and Amy's room, ask him for the placement of a chocolate, and then go back to his own room to find it. In this way Bob gives his young son both a goal and the confidence to move through his blindness.

Bob is also forced to deal with his son. This action brings out something in Bob. He realizes, after a time, that self-hatred has blinded him just as surely as the brigands have blinded his son, that he needs a method like the one he's set up for Lyle to face the killers of his family.

This device is an example of the blending of different elements of fiction writing. Initially, we have the frightened character traits and the responses of Bob and Lyle to the big event at the beginning of the story. Lyle is blind. Bob is half blind and unable even to look at his torturers. Lyle wants sweet chocolate because it is something that gives him solace. Bob wants to rid himself of his bitterness against life.

Later, Bob comes to see that he has abandoned Lyle, whom he has raised as a son even if they aren't related by blood. He uses his intimacy with the boy, made concrete by the chocolate and the layout of their house, to reach him. This action allows Bob to see himself. And maybe it allows Ramona to see something deeper in this taciturn, seemingly cowardly man.

From this point Bob at least understands what he has to do about his fainting spells at the jailhouse and in the court. Will he do it? That will have to come later.

So here we begin to see how the various elements of fiction writing come together in plot. We have started a story with a horrific event that engages the reader's interest. We have gotten to know the main characters through their responses to that event and their relationships to one another. What we have learned about these characters later allows us to understand their struggles with their physical and psychological wounds.

How, and at what moment in the story, these character and story elements are revealed or advanced makes up the plot of your novel. Without this structure, your story may well be flaccid and uninteresting.

✻　　　✻　　　✻

There is another important component to plot that you must always consider: with plot you always have the potential for the element of surprise. You give the reader all the constituent parts of the tale, and then you add these factors together, coming up with an obvious but wholly surprising piece of knowledge or event.

The best way to understand this potential strength of surprise in plot is to look at the structure of most jokes. In a joke you are given a great deal of storylike information up front, but by the end that information comes together in an altogether unexpected way. For example:

A poor woman, with a great big bag of money, goes to a bank officer wanting to make a deposit. When the handsome and arrogant banker asks her how she made her money, she says, "By making bets."

It is a great deal of money, and the banker is dubious. He asks, "What kind of bets?"

She says, "Well, for instance, I might bet you one hundred thousand dollars that you have square testicles."

"You would make that bet?" the banker asks.

The old woman nods.

"For a hundred thousand?" The banker reaches for his zipper.

"Wait," the woman says. "Anyone knows that for a bet to be valid, you have to have a witness."

"I'll call my secretary," the bank officer offers.

"No, no, no," the old woman says. "She works for you. We

must have someone beyond reproach. Do you know the lawyer across the street? The man named Morton?"

"Why, yes," the banker says. "Frank Morton is the most respected jurist in town."

The old woman smiles and says for him to call Morton and have him in his office tomorrow at nine.

The next day the three meet in the banker's office. The old woman says, "Okay, let's see what you got."

The banker drops his pants and grins.

"Pay up," he says.

"Oh," the woman says, a little dismayed, "yes. They seem to be . . . round."

"You better believe it!" the banker confirms.

"Then let me touch them to be sure that they are flesh. Let me hold them in my hand."

The banker balks, but then the thought of all that money steels him. He nods, and the old woman gently cups her hand around his most delicate place.

The moment she touches the banker, the lawyer faints dead away.

"They are truly not square," she says with certainty. "I suppose I must pay you."

"What's wrong with him?" the banker asks.

"Oh," the old woman answers, "yesterday I bet him two hundred thousand dollars that you would willingly let an old woman like me caress you in this most intimate way."

This joke uses a kind of sleight of hand to distract the audience's attention. While we are concentrating on the sexual element of the tale, something else is happening. We have all the information to figure out the punch line, but most of us miss it because of the subterfuge.

The plot in many stories often works the same way. We are waylaid by bright lights and whistles while the real story is unfolding under our noses. When we see the truth of the situation, we are both surprised and delighted — that is, if the method of revelation seems natural and unforced. If the reader feels that they have been tricked, the structure of the plot will backfire, and your reader will turn away, unsatisfied.

final thoughts on plot and story

I'm very happy to be on the other side of having to write about story and plot, the most abstract and complex interconnected components of fiction writing. These two elements are so closely related that they are very hard to separate. And even now, when I look back over what I have written, I wonder if it has been enough.

So let me leave you with an image that might give you another way of looking at these wedded notions.

If we personify the novel, make it into a being named Marissa Novella, for example, I believe that we can see the complex interworkings of story and plot.

The story is the whole person of Ms. Novella — her voice

and smile; her confusion and brilliance; her walnut-colored eyes and red shoes. Every step and action Marissa takes is what we see as the unfolding narrative. But underneath the flesh is the skeleton that gives her the ability to move. This hidden system, along with many others (including her unconscious drives), informs and empowers Marissa. The plot is invisible to us and to the characters that populate the novel, but at the same time it propels the story, or Novella, that we are enjoying.

And we must remember that there's more than one story and plot in every novel. There are at least as many stories as there are main characters, and each of these stories has to have multiple plots to keep it going—blood and bone, nerve and tissue, forgotten longing and unknown events.

the uses of poetry in fiction writing

Poetry is the fount of all writing. Without a deep understanding of poetry and its practices, any power the writer might have is greatly diminished.

This truth I hold to be self-evident.

But I'll try to explain anyway.

Of all writing, the discipline in poetry is the most demanding. You have to learn how to distill what you mean into the most economic and at the same time the most elegant and accurate language. In poetry you have to see language as both music and content. A poet must be the master of simile, metaphor, and form, and of the precise use of vernacular and grammar, implication and innuendo. The poet has to be able to create symbols that are muted and yet undeniable. The poet, above all other writers, must know how to edit out the extraneous, received, repetitious, and misleading. A poet will ask herself, "Why did I use that word, and how will that usage affect meaning later in the poem when that same word is used again? A similar word?"

The poet seeks perfection in every line and sentence; she demands flawlessness of form.

If the fiction writer demands half of what the poet asks of herself, then that writer will render an exquisitely written novel.

When I studied creative writing at the City College of New York (CCNY) in Harlem, I took a poetry workshop every semester. Out of a total of six semesters, I took five with the great departed American poet William Matthews. I don't think I missed any of Bill's classes, but I still can't write even a passable poem.

I am not a poet. My sensibilities do not lie in that direction. But in those three years, Bill taught me how to appreciate the subtleties of language in a way no fiction writing workshop could have addressed. He talked about rhyme, alliteration, assonance, repetition, meter, the music of language, and the need to rewrite again and again until not even one word is out of place.

Bill, and my fellow students, showed me how deeply one could get into an arcane subject with just a hundred words, maybe less.

If you have the chance and the time, I suggest you begin reading poetry. If there's an open evening, join a poetry workshop. You don't have to be good at it. Your poems can be bad. But what you will learn will include all the tools that can stand you in good stead when it comes to writing that novel you intend to finish this year.

3.

Where to Begin

congratulations

You now have all the information you need to write the first draft of your novel. You may have to reread the previous pages a few times. You may have to go out and take a run or get a massage (whatever it is you do to work off anxiety), but you're ready.

Now let's get on with putting your book down in words.

first words

Probably the highest hurdle for the novice novelist (and many seasoned veterans) is writing the first few words. That beginning is a very emotional moment for most of us.

There are all kinds of ways for people to cajole themselves

into starting their book. Some get a special pen or a particular desk set at a window looking out on something beautiful. Others play a favorite piece of music, light a candle, burn incense, or set up some other ritual that makes them feel empowered and optimistic.

If this is what you find you must do to write — well . . . okay. Rituals frighten me. I worry that if I need a special pen or desk or scent to start me out, what will happen when I lose that pen or I'm on vacation or a business trip and my window looks out on the city dump?

My only ritual for writing is that I do it every morning. I wake up and get to work. If I'm in a motel in Mobile — so be it. If I am up all night, and morning is two o'clock in the afternoon, well, that's okay too.

The only thing that matters is that you write, write, write. It doesn't have to be good writing. As a matter of fact, almost all first drafts are pretty bad. What matters is that you get down the words on the page or the screen — or into the tape recorder, if you work like that.

Your first sentence will start you out, but don't let it trip you up.

If you are the intuitive type, just sit down and start writing the novel:

> *Lamont had only enough cash to buy half a pint of whiskey at Bobo's Liquor Emporium, but he knew it wouldn't be enough.*

Ragman was dead, and that was at least a quart's worth of mourning.

What does it mean? How should I know? Those were the first words that came out. I'm not going to worry about it; I'm just going to keep on writing until either something clicks or I lose momentum. If it doesn't seem to be working, I'll start with a new first sentence. I'll keep on like that until something strikes my fancy and I have enough of a handle on the story to continue.

The next morning I read what I wrote the day before, making only the most superficial changes, and then continue on my way. This is all you have to do. Sit down once a day to the novel and start working without internal criticism, without debilitating expectations, without the need to look at your words as if they were already printed and bound.

The beginning is only a draft. Drafts are imperfect by definition.

If you are the structured kind of writer, you might start by getting the outline of your novel down on paper. You know the story already, but now you have to get it down scene after scene, chapter after chapter.

Every day, you sit down, just like the intuitive writer, writing what it is you think your story is about. You discover new characters, add little thumbnail sketches of them; you make notes about the feeling you want to get here and there. You create the whole book out of bulleted phrases and sentences, paragraphs and maybe even flowcharts.

Finally the day will arrive when you come to the end of the outline. The story is set, at least theoretically, and now you must follow the road that the intuitive writer takes. You sit down with your outline somewhere in the room and start writing the prose. You begin with a sentence and keep on going. Maybe you will follow the plan assiduously; maybe you will be diverted onto another path that will lead you far from your original ideas.

Whatever the case, the work is the same. Some days will be rough, unbearable; some will be sublime. Pay no attention to these feelings. All you have to do is write your novel this year. Happy or sad, the story has to come out.

Stick to your schedule. Try to write a certain amount every day—let's say somewhere between 600 and 1,200 words. Do not labor over what's been written. Go over yesterday's work cursorily to reorient yourself, then move on. If you find at some point that you have lost the thread of your story, take a few days to reread all you have written, not with the intention of rewriting (though a little editing is unavoidable) but with the intention of refamiliarizing yourself with the entire work.

Using this method, you should have a first draft of the novel in about three months. It won't be publishable. It won't be pretty. It probably won't make logical sense. But none of that matters. What you will have in front of you is the heart of the book that you wish to write.

There is no greater moment in the true writer's life.

Your first draft is like a rich uncultivated field for the farmer: it is waiting for you to bring it into full bloom.

the midlands of the novel

The beginning of the novel is hard, but it's only a few sentences and you're off on your tale. The end is also difficult because it has to make sense out of all that's gone before. In the rewriting phase of your process, you may spend weeks worrying over a satisfying end point.

But despite all this, it is the middle of your novel, that great expanse of storytelling, that is the most difficult part. How, you ask yourself, do I keep the story going for all those hundreds of pages?

What you have to remember is that a novel is the one and the many. There is an overarching story, and then there are all the smaller narratives that come together to make up that larger tale.

So in the case of Bob, Ramona, and Lyle, we have many bases to cover before we can come to a satisfying conclusion. Ramona must come into sync (through conflict) with Bob and Lyle; the same is true for Lyle and his father. We also have the police, the criminals, the judicial system, and Bob's in-laws to understand. Each character and element involved in the circumstances of this tragedy must be plumbed for us to understand and feel the evolution of that character—especially Bob's.

Keeping these notions in mind, you will find that the novel in some important way writes itself. You know the characters; you know the circumstances—now you must make sure that the reader is aware of every factor that makes up the tale.

You will find yourself in the cell with more than one murderer. You will find yourself in Bob's and Lyle's memories of their lost family members. You will experience the police officers' exasperation with Bob's apparent cowardice. You will come to understand Bob's loveless life, and then you will see how, in a very different way, Ramona has always sought after love.

And with each one of these substories, more of the larger tale will be revealed. Is it a story of forgiveness or retribution, a slow death or a rebirth?

The midlands of your novel can be treacherous, but the map is in the beginning of your story, where the characters are introduced and the conflict occurs. How this conflict is resolved is the content of your tale. There are many strands that must come together into a whole cloth—this is your novel.

research

There will be moments when you will want to dally over details. Do Georgia geese fly south in April or June? Is it physically possible for Bob Millar to hear the cult leader yelling from a mile away—even in a desert? Would the police arrest Trip if the women were allowed into the bar and were served by the owner?

All of these questions are valid. Before the book gets into print, you should have the answers. But many writers allow questions like these to help them procrastinate. They tell themselves that they can't go on until these questions are answered.

Nonsense. Put a red question mark next to the place where you have questions and get back to it later.

I almost always do the research for my books toward the end of the last draft. By that time I know the book is written and that my creative energies will not be sapped by needless fretting.

I have to admit that I'm not the best source when it comes to research. It's not one of my strong suits. I write books about places I've been and people I like to think I understand.

I've known writers who have spent years in libraries and foreign lands researching the topics of their novels. There's nothing I can say about that. If you need to go to South Africa for a month (or five years) to get the feeling for your book, then do it. When you come back and you're ready to write, my little how-to book will be waiting for you. Then you can take the year necessary to write the novel.

4.

Rewriting, or Editing

the first draft

This section marks the borderline between the potential novel and the actual work of art. You have spent three months or more getting down the words. Every day you have planted your backside in a chair for an hour and a half or more and written this novel of yours. Now that you have come to the end of the book, you are ready to write it.

The pages you have stacked neatly in front of you represent what is commonly known as a first draft. It's probably not very good, but that's to be expected. Without a first draft, there would be no novel, so this is without a doubt the most important accomplishment of the writer.

the second draft

Now read your book from first page to last. If you find that you must make pencil markings, correct spelling, add missing words, retool sentences ... be my guest. It doesn't matter what you do as long as you read the entire novel.

This exercise is a very important moment for the novelist. It is a time of discovery. You think you know what you've written, but you find—all through the text—phrasings, words, metaphors, notions, and even evolving themes that lead you to wonder about developing these ideas further. You find mistakes that seem to make sense. You see ideas you once thought profound that now seem petty or trite.

The reason you find so many new things in the draft you have just written is that two people were at work on your book. The first one was you—the person who sat down every morning with coffee on the table and birds chattering outside the window. *You* wrote this novel, every word of it, but still you find surprises and glimmers of things partially forgotten or maybe even ideas that are wholly foreign to you, as if someone else were suggesting them.

That someone else is the you who lives inside, a shadow being that has been brought partially to consciousness by that daily exercise of writing—an exercise, when done in an unrestrained manner, that exhorts unconscious materials. This other side of your awareness may have left vestiges of thoughts, ideas, and feelings long forgotten. These treasures will be scattered among the pages of the draft you have only just completed.

When you have finished reading, you have finished the second draft of your book. Yes, the mere act of reading makes a second draft. Now you have seen what it is that you created. The book has become something more than you ever expected and something less than you intended. You are aware of problems in structure, language, and character development. Good. You are beginning to see other ideas that might be exploited. Even better.

How long should this reading take? I don't know exactly. You will read your own draft faster than you would something wholly new to you, but it will still take time. Let's give it a week. Your work schedule will remain the same, the same amount of time at the same hour — every day.

This is a good time to reiterate the importance of the writer's schedule. You should write *every day*, Monday through Sunday. If you finish the first draft on a Tuesday, then you should begin the second draft (which is reading the first draft) on Wednesday. And, while we're at it, there are no vacations from writing. If you find yourself on holiday in Bermuda, work on your novel every morning instead of reading someone else's book. If you have a toothache, put your protagonist in the dentist's chair. If you fall in love, make that love an aspect of a character in your book. Don't stop writing for any reason. Don't stop writing. Don't stop. . . . Don't.

*　　*　　*

You have spent around twelve weeks writing the first draft and now another week acquainting yourself with the work, and its writer, as a whole. Thirteen weeks—one-quarter of a year exactly.

The time is getting short.

the many drafts that follow

Now begins the hard work. Now you have to go through your book idea by idea, character by character, chapter by chapter, paragraph by paragraph, sentence by sentence, and finally even word by word, submitting it to many, many levels of analysis and critique.

In the early rewriting drafts, you will make notes about the problems you perceived in the novel in that first all-important reading. Does the story engage you? Does the story make sense? Have you set up a pattern of revelation (the plot) that moves the story along? Is there any discernible change in the main character(s)? And how do the ideas that manifested themselves in the second draft affect how you see the story now?

The first draft of the novel may have been written in many different ways (e.g., typewritten, entered on a computer, scribbled in pencil), but now you need a printed version of the book (preferably double-spaced) and a pencil with a fresh eraser. You need a stack of blank paper that you will use to make notes, lists, internal schedules, and longer insertions.

You will need that time each day and absolute silence because now is when you become Sisyphus rolling that impossible weight up the hill. Any distraction might well cause a misstep, and you will lose control.

What should be your plan? How should you go about reworking the manuscript in front of you until it is a finished book?

There are different ways to approach this job, but there is one that all writers have in common: you must decide whether or not this document is worth the next nine months of your life.

I'm not asking you if the book is pretty, well tooled, sensible, or even mostly comprehensible. What you have to decide here is whether the novel has a soul or not. Is there a story in all that mangled-up language that is worth the telling?

This may take another reading, and one after that. Each of these can be considered a draft. Roll past the inelegant phrasings and contradictory timing. Ignore the plot flaws and hackneyed notions. Love isn't articulate at first blush. Neither are most important ideas.

Look closely at your book and make sure that you want to see the novel it implies.

Once you have made this decision, there are different paths you can take. These paths are many, but all can be reached through either the intuitive or the structured approach.

You may wish to start on page one, retooling sentences and setting up the theme at the same time. You might decide to go through the novel making only certain kinds of changes (e.g., dialogue tooling, spelling, word repetition) and making notes for future drafts when other issues arise.

Whatever choice you make, tomorrow is when you begin the next nine months of draft making.

the elements of rewriting

In this section I will give you an idea of what is possible to attain in the process of rewriting, along with a few suggestions about what you should be looking for when you're trying to make a better story.

the nexus of character, story, theme, and plot

When the writer began telling the story about Marissa and Love, she was under the impression that Love was just an overbearing force standing in the path of her daughter's personal development. Maybe this writer was thinking about her own mother, or other older women she'd known who had been impediments while professing to have concern for her.

When going over the story, the writer realizes that Love has a static character. She makes no transition in the telling of the tale, but she is obviously an important player therein.

This is a problem that the novelist jots down. "What to do about Love's character development?" she scribbles at the bottom of page 180.

Later, on the ninth rereading, a line pops out at the rewriter. Let's say that Trip has been released from jail, and even though he has been having an affair with Marissa's best friend, Marissa takes him back.

Enraged at her daughter, Love says, "Man's just a wild dog without a leash."

This declaration doesn't make sense; of course a wild dog doesn't have a leash. The first consideration is to delete this bit of dialogue. But then again . . . *maybe Marissa will see that the phrase makes no sense and learn something about her mother.*

This idea seems good. The author adds the thought into Marissa's internal dialogue. But later the writer comes across the note about Love's character. This brings her back to wild dogs with no leashes — what could she have meant? The statement is not really in character for Love; she'd more likely say, "That Trip's a wild dog that should be put down." But instead she wants him on a leash. . . .

When no answer comes, the rewriter leaves this problem and goes on retooling sentences and looking for overused words. Then, a week or so later, she comes back to the wild-dog declaration. Love seems to be worried about Trip; she's thinking that Marissa doesn't know how to deal with a man like him. Maybe she believes that Trip will be harmed by a woman who doesn't know how to grab hold of her man and make him see that he's not some damned cowboy on TV.

If this is so, maybe Love has a backstory—a time when she loved someone too much—and maybe she believes that this uncontrolled love killed her man. Love killed her man. This sentence takes on a double meaning. Love's relationship to her daughter now makes sense, her hatred of Trip is somewhat clearer, and a possibility for her to learn something (or at least to recognize that thing) opens the potential for her character to change as the story unfolds.

Love's story might be the underlying theme of the novel. Maybe the characters are seeing themselves in their loved ones and not loving them for who they are.

The story started out as a tale about a young woman who was hindered by those who professed love but did not deliver. But now, after this wild-dog notion, we see Marissa in a new way. Rather than being the personification of innocence, she begins to represent danger. Love and Trip become her victims. So instead of the original trite ending—the one in which Marissa moves to Phoenix and falls in love with her rich and handsome boss—we see Marissa at the cemetery, where, on that same day, funerals are being held for both her lover and her mother.

The novel changes course from romance to black comedy, and we begin to tease out moments in Marissa's life that seem innocent but when added up equal an unconscious force of nature that overwhelms everyone and everything around her.

This, I believe, is a good example of what can come from rewriting. Our questioning of every phrase and every element of the novel will blend together and bond into a story that will do us well.

the devil and the details

The above example illustrates the most important overarching concerns in any successful rewrite: What is the novel about? How do the characters come together and change? What does it all mean?

These large notions are important, but if you don't write a reader-friendly book, no one is ever going to get that far.

The following are the minutiae of rewriting any piece of prose.

repetition

First, you must cut out all extraneous repetition of words and phrases. Punctilious, pinewood table, amber eyed, flatulent, moribund . . . these words, and most others, should hardly ever be repeated within a few pages of one another. To go even further, they shouldn't be used more than two or three times in the whole book.

Repetition, as any poet can tell you, is employed to bring attention to the word or phrase being used. Maybe the word has more than one meaning (e.g., "Love" as a name and an emotion). Maybe it echoes a deep emotional state. "Death all around me—Death, with its sightless eyes and mirthless grins; Death, with its silent tales and broken promises; Death, that eternal visitor, who came to my mother and father and theirs and theirs and theirs."

If you're going to repeat a word or phrase, have a reason for it. Maybe it's used to create a mood or to underline deep desire. Maybe your use of repetition will show you something about the story; if not, get rid of it. If the repeated word seems necessary, open a thesaurus and find a synonym. If there is no appropriate equivalent, rewrite the sentence. And if the sentence refuses to be rewritten . . . well, okay, you can use the repetition—but just this once.

descriptions and condensation

Any simple act or situation in life is comprised of hundreds of actions and circumstances. Just look around the room you're in—the number of chairs, tables, and paintings on the wall; the subject of those paintings; the color of the wall or carpet; the aberrations inside those colors. There might be a fly buzzing overhead or a dead mosquito amid clumps of dust in the corner behind the couch. What is the temperature of the room? How many people are there? Are the ceilings high?

Low? Is it a large room? Are there sounds other than the fly in the room? Are there sounds from the outside? The people might be talking. Do you understand them? No? Why not? Is it because they are murmuring or because they are speaking a foreign language? (Maybe you don't hear as well as you once did.) What kind of clothes are they wearing?

These are more or less objective observations of the place one might be in. But now that person takes an action. Let's say that he picks up a cup of coffee (by the handle or the body?) and drinks from it. Is the coffee hot? Tepid? Cold?

The character is sitting across from someone, a woman he's interested in. What is she wearing? How old is she? What is her expression? What irregularities are there in her skin?

You could go on forever. Details are endless, and they will overwhelm your story unless you master them. Even the most interesting acts cannot bear the weight of too much detail.

Let's say that the man and the woman leave the public hall and go upstairs to the bedroom. They begin to make love. Their progress in this will seem endless if you record every action taken. He puts a hand on her shoulder. She looks away. He touches her forearm and notices a dark cloud out the north-facing window. She caresses his right cheek with the palm of her left hand. They stare into each other's eyes. . . . Sixteen pages later, they're getting ready for their second kiss.

Details will devour your story unless you find the words that want saying.

*   *   *

The only details that should be put in any description are those that advance the story or our understanding of the character. The only details that should be put in any description are those that advance the story or our understanding of the character. (You see—repetition works.) So when the main character, Van, walks into the room, he's nervous about talking to Rena, the woman he's interested in. Maybe the fly manifests Van's anxiety. He notices its lonely buzzing in the big empty space of the ceiling, by the pastoral scenes of the paintings on the wall, and onto the wedding ring, which glints like an amber fog light from his finger.

You might use other details, but here again they should be used only to further story or plot, character development, or the mood of the scene.

The room is warm. Van knows this even though he's feeling chilled. He knows because of the three beads of sweat on Rena's forehead. The murmuring of the men sitting two tables away makes Van nervous. He wonders what they're saying. He tries so hard to make out their words that he misses what Rena has just said.

The awareness of details comes into the novel via the experiences and emotional responses of your characters. Using this as your rule of thumb, you can cut out most extraneous facets in any scene.

But there's another level of description and condensation that you must be aware of—you should not confuse the reader's understanding of character responses with overly ornate and ambivalent detail.

Van was irate, angry, furious, out of his mind with rage.

Here the fledgling writer is trying to build a mood by using three different words and one phrase that convey similar meanings. Each word is more powerful than its predecessor until we come upon a six-word saying to cap off the sentence.

The problems with using this kind of language and structure to explain Van's feeling are threefold. First, the words are at odds with one another. Is Van angry or out of his mind with rage? Is he furious or irate? Second, even if we accept all the words as a buildup to a kind of personified explosion, we still have to wonder at those aspects of the definition of each word that make what is being said a kind of repetition. It's always best to give the reader one emotional state at a time to deal with.* The third problem with this description of Van's fury is the question of who it is that's giving us the information—even an omniscient narrator wouldn't be so removed from the character's heart as to use this objective, albeit strong, language. The description of Van's anger feels like an out-of-kilter definition rather than a closely felt experience.

So how do we fix this sentence? There are many ways. If

---

*That is, unless the character really is having ambivalent or conflicting emotions.

the only thing that bothers you is the narrative voice, you might want to change the declarative sentence into a bit of dialogue. Maybe Rena, after seeing Van obliterate that annoying fly with the flat of his hand, tells a friend what she thought Van was feeling. Depending on her character, this sentence might work well. Dialogue can be sloppy, overly elaborate, inarticulate, and many other things that the novel's narrative voice can never afford to be. If we believe that Rena communicates in this repetitious manner, we will accept the information and move on without question.

We could get rid of all the adjectives and simply show Van smashing the fly and then looking at the remains of the insect with grim satisfaction.

We might have Van say something over the top and inappropriate for this seduction scene.

"I hate that goddamned fly."

The easiest thing to do is to get rid of the sentence and go on. Maybe his rage or anger or fury is not all that important to the story.

Always try to pare down the language of your novel. Is that word necessary? That sentence, that paragraph, that chapter? Most writers tend to overwrite. They either fall in love with their use of language or want to make sure that the reader understands everything.

But, as we saw above, you can never say everything. There

are too many details in reality. Fiction is a collusion between the reader and the novel. If you have brought your characters into the story in such a way that their emotions both color and define their world, you will find that readers will go along with you — creating a much larger world as they do. It won't be exactly the world you intended them to see, but it will be close enough — sometimes it will be better.

You must investigate each sentence, asking yourself, "Does it make sense? Does it convey the character properly? Does it generate the right mood? Is it too much? Does it get the narrative voice right?"

Every sentence.

Every sentence.

dialogue

How your characters express themselves is just as important as what they say.

> *"Man walk up to me," Roger said, "an' say he know my name . . . I told him he better get on outta here."*

We know a great deal about Roger from just this snippet of dialogue. He's angry and confrontational. He might be afraid of something, and he identifies himself with a street sensibility. He probably isn't well educated, but he has a subtle appreciation of language. We understand that Roger's dialogue has the potential to tell us things he doesn't say.

> *"What's wrong?" Benny asked Minna.*
> *"Nothing."*
> *"Come on," he said, coaxing her by touching the side of her hand with a single finger.*
> *"Um . . ."*

Here we appreciate an underlying disturbance in Minna. Benny sees it and tells us about it as he questions his friend and reaches out to her. He has seen beneath her subterfuge. It might be that these few words are intended to tell us about the relationship between these two rather than to lead us to some undisclosed personal problem.

Many new writers use dialogue to communicate information such as "My name is Frank. I come from California." This is the simplest use of dialogue. It's okay for a job interview or a chance meeting in a bar, but in the novel, dialogue is meant to be working overtime.

Every time characters in your novel speak, they should be: (1) telling us something about themselves; (2) conveying information that may well advance the story line and/or plot; (3) adding to the music or the mood of the scene, story, or novel; (4) giving us a scene from a different POV (especially if the character who is speaking is not connected directly to the narrative voice); and/or (5) giving the novel a pedestrian feel.

Most of these points are self-explanatory. The last two, however, are worth a closer look.

If your novel is written in the first or third person, you have a little extra work to do with those characters who are communicating most directly with the reader. A first-person narrator, for instance, might not be aware of certain aspects of her personality or the effect her presence has on others. The writer wants her to be humble in this way and therefore brings in another character to say what the narrator cannot say (or maybe even know) about herself.

> *"They all love you," Leonard told me. "Everybody does. Markham said that the only way they'd let me come was if I brought you along."*

The narrator could deny what Leonard has told her. Later on we will be able to tell if he was right or wrong.

Making the dialogue pedestrian might seem counterproductive to the passionate writer. Here you are, telling us a story of profound feeling in which the main characters are going to experience deeply felt transitions, and I'm asking you for ordinary and prosaic dialogue.

Absolutely.

If you can get the reader to identify with the everydayness

of the lives of these characters and *then* bring them—both reader and character—to these rapturous moments, you will have fulfilled the promise of fiction. The reader is always looking for two things in the novel: themselves and transcendence. Dialogue is an essential tool to bring them there.

Among the five points, there isn't anything all that challenging. I'm sure the new writer will have no difficulty getting a secondary character to interact with the first-person narrator, giving us much-needed information. It's not that hard to put plot points into someone's mouth. . . .

The problem is getting three or more of our five rules working at the same time. The problem is making sure that when Leonard is telling us something about the first-person narrator, he's also telling us something about himself *and* advancing the plot.

> *"They all love you, not me," Leonard said. "Markham didn't care that I stole that money for him. He told me I could get lost if I didn't bring you with me. You're the only one him and his crowd want to see."*

Inside this dialogue there is jealousy, hints of self-deprecation, the fact that Leonard is a criminal, *and* the impact that the narrator has on others.

The information in this example might be too blunt. But I'm sure you see what I mean. Dialogue in your novel is not just characters talking. It is sophisticated fiction.

❊   ❊   ❊

There are many different ways to get people to speak in novels. They can have conversations, write and read letters, and leave messages on answering machines; someone can tell one person something that someone else has said; one character can overhear someone else's conversation. People shout, whisper, lie, seem to be saying one thing when they're saying something else.

Dialogue is an endless pleasure, but you have to get it right.

Do not attempt to use slang or dialect unless you are 100 percent sure of the usage. If you get it wrong, it will taint the entire book. In relation to this admonition, remember that "less is more" when you're dealing with accents, dialect, and colloquial speech.

"Yeah, I seen 'im."

If you're sure about this articulation, then use it, but consider completing the idea through explanation rather than dialect.

"Yeah, I seen 'im," Bobby Figueroa said. Then he told me that Susan's brother was on the lookout for Johnny Katz.

As they say in boxing, "Protect yourself at all times." If you aren't sure about the way someone will say something, then find another way to get at the same idea.

❋ ❋ ❋

One final note about dialogue: a novel is not a play. Don't house your entire story in conversations. Don't try to contain the whole plot in dialogue. As with metaphor, overuse of dialogue can bewilder and distance your reader from the experience of the novel.

a solitary exercise

In your meticulous rewrite, one problem you will be looking for is flatness in the prose.

> *I went to the store and bought a dozen apples. After that I came home and decided to call Marion. She told me that she was busy and so she couldn't make it to the dance.*

I won't try to rewrite this flaccid prose for you. I'm sure by this time you can see the various ways that you might approach the revision. So instead I will ask you to take these three sentences and make them into something more.

Consider the character who is speaking, the potential drama behind Marion's reason for not going to the dance, the missing details, and the misconnections. From this, make the lines into some kind of beginning for a novel. Don't write more than a page. Pretend that it was written by some writer friend who wants to tell a story but has gotten lost somehow.

I'm not much for giving exercises. I believe that the novel itself is your exercise. But in this case there is a reason.

Most writers, especially new writers, can see the problems in other people's prose while being blind to their own failings. This exercise should be an experience that you will keep in mind while working on the revision of your own book.

music

Language and song are mingled in human history. To speak, to sing, is our heritage. Poets know that poems are songs, but few of us realize that novels are too. If there is no music to your novel, no sound, then the book will be at best incomplete. You must have a rhythm to your characters, a unique cadence to the way each one speaks, an identifiable cacophony to the world(s) they inhabit, and a beat to the story that, when varied, gives the reader an almost unconscious sign of events about to unfurl.

Novels, like large musical pieces, have movements. But unlike an opera or symphony, the novel doesn't have set notation and rules for its musicality. There's no score. There is no set theory for the music of prose. These truths are at once daunting and exciting. No one will tell you how to score your novel, so that means you have to discover the music for yourself.

"How can I do that?" you might well ask.

The answer is simple. Buy a tape recorder, and when you've

done all the rewriting you can stand, read your book out loud into the little microphone — yes, the whole book. It will take you seven or eight morning sessions, but it will be worth it. When you listen to yourself while reading, when you play back the words you read, the sound of the characters and their world will come to you. You will understand how you want Aunt Angie to sound. You will see what was missing from those scenes on the street. You will remember birds and transistor radios and the blustering walruslike attitude of the surly man who saved your protagonist's life.

A tape recording of your book will do more than help with the will-o'-the-wisp musicality of the piece; it will also help you see things that you missed while rereading silently. You will detect words and phrasings that are wrong, misplaced, and overly used. You will become aware of giant plot gaffes and a plethora of misspellings. This is because, after rewriting for a while, you begin to know what you are (re)reading without actually reading it. You overlook mistakes because you know what you meant.

I cannot stress how important this recording can be to your work. Maybe you are in the fortieth week of the book. This is the moment to reconsider and reflect on what you've done. The tape recorder is a perfect test for the worth, and the music, of your work.

If you don't want to record the book (or if you can't afford or borrow a tape recorder), you can still get a lot out of reading out loud to yourself. This exercise alone will allow you to experience the story another way.

You could, if you have very patient friends or loved ones, read out loud to one or more of them. You don't have to read much. Just five pages will be invaluable to your rewrite.

when am I finished rewriting?

Never. The novel never attains the level of perfection. No matter how much you rewrite and rewrite again, you will still find places in the book that don't do exactly what you want. You will feel that some characters are hazy, and plot connections unsure. There's a subplot that will seem to get lost and a fairly important character that will change but not as much as you might have wished.

This is true for all writers in all forms. Books are not pristine mathematical equations. They are representative of humanity and are therefore flawed.

"So when will I know to stop rewriting?" you ask.

When you see the problems but, no matter how hard you try, you can't improve on what you have. That's it. You find yourself reading through the book for the twenty-fifth time, and as you see problems, you try to fix them, but the attempt only makes things worse. . . . Then you know you're finished.

Congratulations. You have a novel. This one is good. The next one will be better.

5

Miscellany

on genre

A novel is a novel is a novel. A crime story is a novel. A romance is a novel. A book about aliens that came to Earth millennia ago and made us what we are is also a novel. Most books have elements of crime, mystery, romance, and the fabulous to them. No one who is serious about literature would dismiss *One Hundred Years of Solitude* for being a fantasy. No one would write off *The Stranger* because of its courtroom or crime details.

All novels have similar elements. They have a beginning, middle, and end. They have characters who change and a story that engages; they have a plot that pushes the story forward and a sound that insinuates a world.

In these ways all novels are the same, but if you take on

the task of writing inside a particular genre, you will do well to pay attention to the conventions of that kind of book. A mystery, for instance, usually has a complex plot that engages much of the reader's attention. Where is the missing girl? Who killed Cock Robin? The story here is, in large part, about a conundrum surrounding a crime. But you still have character development and ideas, relationships and themes.

A romance novel is about the complications and heart-break of love. This genus of fiction pays close attention to relationships, their impossibility, and their transcendence. Again, only part of the novel concentrates on these issues—the rest of the book is a story like any other.

Westerns are about a place and time and the people who lived then. Science fiction speculates on what we might know in the future based on what we do know today. Courtroom thrillers need a trial and lawyers and judges, law enforcement, and an accused.

If you take on a genre, you should know something about the form, but you shouldn't let the form gain greater importance than the novel itself. All novels are about characters and their transitions based on the story being revealed through a precise plot.

a note on aesthetics

You may have come to this book with high literary aspirations and ambitions. You may have read Ellison and Bellow,

Morrison and Melville. You may have wanted your novel to enter into a dialogue with these great literary lights. And so when you perused the previous pages, you may have been a little let down. Perhaps you were looking for an epiphany, and all you found was a joke.

If you find that the previous paragraph expresses your feelings, I say, "Do not despair." This book is meant only to teach the rudiments of novel writing. Greatness lies in the heart of the writer, not in technique. A great novel does not have to be the work of a consummate wordsmith. A flawless literary technician will not necessarily create works of art.

Even if you are destined to be a critically acclaimed writer, you will still need to learn the lessons rendered here. All I can provide are the bricks and mortar; the architectural design, and its art, must come from you.

writing workshops

Writing workshops are useful to many. I'm not sure if they are necessary for anyone. Trial and error is how we learn. Workshops are based on failed experiments. You bring in your story or chapter, and everyone, regardless of his or her level of expertise, weighs in on what you did right and wrong.

Some of the criticism may be accurate; some might be completely off. But no matter what anyone says, it will not be your own idea, so you will have to keep those external notions at bay.

The thing I found the most useful about criticism in writing workshops was what people, especially the instructor, said about the problems in *other students'* work. These constructive analyses of other people's writing were objective inasmuch as I didn't have anything at stake but was likely to have the same problems in my own work.

You can learn some things in a classroom situation, but this is not the only use for the writing workshop. The two most valuable benefits are interrelated: building community and making possible literary connections.

Writing in America can be a lonely experience. It is not a revered occupation (unless you write the script for some blockbuster movie). Most Americans are not interested in the unpublished writer. If you say you write, they ask, "Are you published?"

But in a writing workshop, everyone is interested in the process of writing and the life of writers. Your comrades in this setting will ask about what you are working on and what you are doing to promote the work. This community-building leads to the second use of the writing workshop: you meet people who are trying to put work out in the world. They talk about literary magazines, agents, publishers, small presses, and so on.

If you are interested in a career as a writer—or just wish to be published now and then—workshops can be very useful.

literary organizations, agents, publishers . . . and getting published

Getting published is another Sisyphean task. You will be rolling your manuscript(s) up and down Publisher's Mountain many a time before you get your first book over the top. At this moment in my career, after publishing twenty-seven books and at least as many short stories, I still get rejected on a regular basis. Recently I wrote a story that every major magazine rejected. After going to the major presses, I went to the smaller ones. Nobody will publish it—nobody.

So don't despair—accepting rejection is part of the job description.

As a published writer, I have no special qualifications that allow me to tell others how to get published. I was studying writing at CCNY when my mentor there, Frederic Tuten, gave the manuscript for *Devil in a Blue Dress* to his agent. She agreed to represent me. This certainly does not make me an expert on publishing strategies.

There are various publications that list all the magazines, agents, and publishers available to writers. There are organizations for every genre: the MWA (Mystery Writers of America), for example, has a newsletter and supports various conventions where workshops are offered on all the issues of the business of mystery writing. The other genres have similar offerings. If you are a student or teacher, there's the AWP (Association of Writers and Writing Programs), which also offers a newsletter and a convention with a ton of informative workshops.

One useful tidbit of information that I can give you is that if you want to publish this novel (the one you wrote this year) with one of the big publishers in New York, you will need a literary agent.

How does one get a literary agent?

The best way is through someone who knows and works with that agent. A personal connection is always best. Failing that, you might, in your perusal of bookstores and libraries, have found certain contemporary novels that have a resonance with your own work. Call the publisher of said work and ask who represents that writer. Get the agent's address and send her or him a query letter explaining who you are (a vitae), what you have written, and how that writing echoes work that the agent has represented. In the best of all possible worlds, that agent will ask you for a sample of your book. After that, keep your fingers crossed.

The only admonition I have is that you should never work with an agent who charges for their services. They should want to make money off the sale of the book, not from you.

6.

In Summation

That's it—everything I know about novel writing in less than 25,000 words. The work is up to you. I'm sure that if you write every day and take these lessons to heart, you will write a novel that works. This process will transform you. It will give you confidence, pleasure, a deeper understanding of how you think and feel; it will make you into an artist and a fledgling craftsperson.

Maybe it will do more.

Index

About the Author

Walter Mosley is the author of numerous bestselling works of fiction and nonfiction, including the acclaimed Easy Rawlins series of mysteries. The first Easy Rawlins novel, *Devil in a Blue Dress*, was made into a feature film starring Denzel Washington and Don Cheadle. Another novel, *Always Outnumbered, Always Outgunned*, for which Mosley received the Anisfield-Wolf Book Award, was made into an HBO feature film starring Laurence Fishburne. His first novel for young-adult readers, *47*, was published in 2005. Walter Mosley was born in Los Angeles and lives in New York.